Arrivals of Light

Robin Fulton Macpherson

ARRIVALS OF LIGHT

Shearsman Books

First published in the United Kingdom in 2020 by
Shearsman Books Ltd
PO Box 4239
Swindon
SN3 9FN

Shearsman Books Ltd Registered Office
30–31 St. James Place, Mangotsfield, Bristol BS16 9JB
(this address not for correspondence)

www.shearsman.com

ISBN 978-1-84861-718-6

Acknowledgements
are due with respect to first publication of certain poems in this
collection: *BABEL; The Dark Horse; Fras; The Glasgow Review of
Books; The Manhattan Review; Northwords Now; painted, spoken;
Shearsman; The Swedish Book Review; Terminus* (Georgia Tech).

Three poems have been published as fine-edition single-poem
booklets: 'An Arrival of Light' from BABEL Verlag, 'String Quartet'
from 13 EDITION, and 'Ålesund Harbour', with Kevin Perryman's
German translations, also from 13 EDITION.

The following were first published (with Kevin Perryman's German
translations) in *13 Poems / 13 Gedichte* designed by Alexandra Frohloff:
'In the Gaze', 'Birthday', 'Shore Wisdom', 'Remembering Mist',
'Whitsun Without Words', 'Far Away is Here' and 'The Light Maker'.

CONTENTS

Twenty-One Miniatures

Afterword

CROWS AND HERON

From the black lace of a leafless birch
seven crows seem to be watching one
heron rowing air from A to B.

On my way past their landscape I'd like
to ask the crows why they haven't moved
and the heron why it's chosen B.

Like an impatient supervisor
my own landscape hurries me forward
fearing I'll leave my long alphabet

uninvested like the one talent
of the unprofitable servant
who was banished to outer darkness.

RUSH-HOUR

Seed wings from plane trees scuttle
like souls across open space,
huddle in lines under walls

as if
where two or three are gathered
there might be hope for millions.

PARALLEL

The universe I live parallel to
has its hard surfaces and timetables.
I have no immunity against them.

In dreams I flow through them as moonlight flows
through the brightest and the darkest shadows
along forest edges and nocturnal shores.

SAME TREE

Driving through mist, through nowhere.
A pine tree, the only one
in the world, in history,
looms over me, leaning in
from its many centuries.

Next day, same road. The tree hides
now one in a crowd. It stares
back at me, is defiant
as if it had never been
to the ends of earth and back.

ABORIGINAL

Recollected or
reinterpreted –
Scotland? Perhaps, if

curlews too distant
and corncrakes too close
to say where they are

but if a gravestone
or two with Macleod,
Sutherland, Shearer

there can't be a perhaps.

IN THE GAZE

The small waves are identical.
They hurry just to get nowhere.
The fjord wants to stay where it is.

The remarkably round beech tree
halfway up the hill is content
to remain remarkably round.

The hill has no wish to be moved.
In the gaze of eternity
fjord, tree, hill – and the man en route –

can't perhaps expect a wide choice.

BIRTHDAY

Dandelions have invaded
all of yesterday's green spaces.
The yellow can't control its rage.

A number is attached to me
for a long race. Where do I run?
I'm trapped in a blind labyrinth
made of invisible hedges.

CLOUD MASTERY

The blue clouds turn the oceans blue.
The green clouds turn the forests green.

Not everything in the heavens,
though, is as the heavens would want.
Spring light landing finally here
seems disappointed: was it worth
the effort to illuminate

neglected backyards, dumped tractors,
dried willow-herb stalks from last year?

LIFE IN THE UNIVERSE

If only the trees would stop rushing past,
stay where they are
so that from a still point I could watch them.

We grow weary balancing on the edge
of ellipses.

DREAM-DOOR

In my dream the door had no lock
no handle.
"You're pushing at an open door"
voices said.
But the door was intractable.

I asked my dream what was beyond
the closed door.
"Cotton-grass by Loch an Ruathair
or perhaps
a harebell by The Pentland Firth."

NASTURTIUM NIGHTMARE

I planted small ones, got big ones:
leaves as wide as wide umbrellas
blocked out my southern horizon
then darkened the highest heavens
with an unfathomable green.

Blossoms shrank to ochre pin-points.
The pin-points shrank into the night.
Watching them I too was a point
perhaps some day detectable
in a fuzz of radio waves.

FROM A VERY HIGH WINDOW

A cloud the length and breadth of Aarhus
half darkens every street in Aarhus,
looks more like a stone lid than soft cloud.

The cathedral, millions of bricks piled
to make us look up, from here is squat.
The tenements know how high they've reached.

The word for spire tries to hide the spire.
The word for cloud tries to hide the cloud.
The word for eye tries to hide the eye.

Beyond the jurisdiction of cloud
there is brightness to be imagined
flowing in oat-fields and forest tops.

SHORE WISDOM

It was the fifth day:
there was agreement
that the deep waters
on the face of Earth
should remain opaque
and teem with knowledge.

At the shallow edge
even of oceans
we see everything:
the stones bulge and shrink
slightly
as the water breathes.

WHERE OLAV H. HAUGE LIVED

At times he found space for them
in three or four lines of verse:
the height of the high rock slabs,
the depth of the deep black fjord.

However few words he used
crag and fjord took their revenge:
the hard crag became higher,
the black fjord became deeper.

AN ARRIVAL OF LIGHT

Still-life with hospital walls,
slabs not built to last long, pocked
already by the present.

I was trapped high above roofs
in a box called Wednesday.
I couldn't cross the chasm
to the next box, called Thursday.
The dream failed to rescue me.

A gash in the cloud-cover
glared me into wakefulness.
Sunlight that travels so far
so fast lands here so gently
as if to persuade me walls
can be made of light, immune
to the corrosions of stone.

A NEW DAY

Dawn was a cramped shadowy room.
I stumbled in with unwieldy baskets
full of the night's dream-detritus.

A voice that sounded like my own
mumbled to me from the inmost corner
"Don't bring your bedlam-baskets here."

A pigeon on someone's roof moaned
"Nowhere to put them, nowhere to put them,
you'd better go back to the dark."

AFTER SOMEONE'S DEATH

They can hold out against September gales,
all those leaves not ready to be scattered.
Each tree has its own voice in the fierce air.

Calendulae, cornflowers and nasturtiums
have followed me for all of my decades.
They wonder if I am ephemeral.

I wonder if the wall we imagine,
the one beyond which we have no knowledge,
is not a wall but a net, filaments,
and the forest wind, its many voices,
without hindrance sweeps to and fro between
a world we can't begin to imagine
and a world we can't imagine forgetting.

FOREST FAREWELL

I'll never say goodbye to the pine-trees
but the pine-trees will say goodbye to me:

"Our silhouettes will not be diminished
and our resin will still smell resinous.
We won't notice leaving you far behind."

SOME THINGS GREAT AND SMALL

Alive, in its way,
a cactus, tiny
as a push-button
and chasms beneath
the attention of
upper pine-levels.

At my own level
my eyes are too big
to see eightsome reels
whirled by particles
in the solid rock
I think I stand on.

ISLAND

Tiny leafed miracles are lodged in seams.
Pines have grown old, like a huge family
never forgetting, always there for us.

We reach the island by sea, leave by sea.
The waves can't stop turning away from us.
They have yet to discover rocks and roots.

THAT LOMBARDY POPLAR

The one no longer there.
An acquaintance of sorts
for decades, then cut down.

Revisiting, decades
on, I walk between staunch
beech boles not yet cut down.

It's the tree no longer
here that feels most present –
like the familiar dead
who're never far away.

STRATH

Decades ago its replica
lodged in my brain made hazel-leaves
scrape like edges of broken glass.

The leaves now sound like leaves again.

The wide cloud-shadows pay no heed
to the cramped shadows in our brains.
They touch each leaf as if healing.

ROOKS, AND OTHERS

Rook-voices full of today,
each young generation loud
with the words of ancestors –
do rooks think, if they do think,
everything they say is new?

Not as when
day after day father parks
his Austin Cambridge between
garden shed and manse back-porch
letting me hear the door thud
clear across six decades. And

not as when
the drifting tobacco smells
of wartime adults still drifts
through today's hawthorn blossom
giving it a moment's scent
of an acrid concentrate.

UNIVERSES

This month the moon's at its fattest
and brightest for three-score-and-nine.
It looks as if it can see more.

This moment a dark speck fidgets
through half-yellow still-hanging-on
hortensia leaves. It's a wren.

A rain-drop survives the shaking
and can still show me a clear curved
private view of its universe.

NOVEMBER DUSK

The day still has eight hours to go
but already it seems finished.

As the evening darkens it spills
more and more light and the light pours
from compass points we've never seen:
they emerge behind the old ones.

Like an Emil Nolde landscape,
so much indigo and scarlet
swirling and leaving no room for
everyday light, everyday dark.

There's more space to get lost in now
that the universe is even bigger.

NOT WHAT WE THOUGHT

Beethoven's improvisation –
played only once, heard only once
perhaps only by Beethoven.

York Minster weighs down and soars up,
has been stared at by centuries,
looks as if it can't stop lasting.

Reality's not what it seems.

There have been persistent rumours
of a cathedral-shaped glimmer
someone perhaps saw, once, in York.

Beethoven's improvisation
from the early 1820s
is new with each repetition.

LOCH AND STAR

The loch once had a Gaelic name
but chose to lose it, preferring
anonymity.
The star which on very clear nights
had a hesitant reflection
never quite whole, never quite lost
in the dim wavelets – it once had
a Latin name but preferred now
to shine without name or number
in a non-heaven.

So many years ago I spent
so many hours out on the loch.
I came away with stillness learnt
from restless water.
And I've dreamt that my passport gives
as my country of residence
a non-country with a non-loch
sometimes reflecting a non-star.
My lips smelled of peaty water
and my hands of trout.

OPUS 106

What if a masterpiece was lost
before anyone could notice
it was masterful? Imagine
ink turning wet again, streaming
like today's rain on the window.

I was about to listen but
closed the score. (Was the autograph
written with home-made ink, or ink
once advertised as "permanent"?)
It's not every day we listen.

It's not every day we're up to
such violence of sunlight, such thrust
as of wedges testing the joints
of small universes we build
to keep rain out, let some light in,
protect whatever warmth there is.

THE SHORTEST DAY

Low cloud makes sure: there are no hills,
trees that once wanted to be tall
have had to stop growing half-way,
the dawn tried to happen but failed.

We are discouraged from thinking
that something like a universe
is making and breaking its rules
about time, somewhere, and shining.

ADAGIO SOSTENUTO

While we're yet in time the passing of time
belongs to a past we don't remember.

We've left words behind the way spring forgets
the soft clink of ice it melted away.

PROBABLY NOT

Too wakeful to the world at large:
distraction decade by decade.
Too many waves in the ocean,
too many trees in the forest,
too many known stars in the sky,
too many unknown stars beyond.

Would it be enough to get by
with only one loch far from roads,
hidden between empty hillsides
and visited hardly ever?
Or one tree, old when I was young
and with luck good for centuries?
Or one simple constellation
keeping its balance above roofs?

LAMP

I pause beneath a street-lamp
in the dark before dawn.
What a narrow world I'm in,
neither bright nor shaded,
an unchanging amber glow
on asphalt without news
but for the arrival and
departure of moisture.

What a wide world of darkness
the lamp closes from us.
The weak lamp gets the better
of a black universe
eager for the end of light.

STRING QUARTET

The listeners can listen
if they want.
They stand outside like tall
patient trees.

Inside walls and windows
four players
breathe as if sharing one
deathless lung.

They need no audience.
Their music
has no knowledge of walls
or windows,

becomes a wide forest.
Each leaf breathes
like no other. The leaves
breathe as one.

SUN THROUGH MIST

Normal life has been persuaded
not to be normal.
Colours have been told to calm down.

As if a horizon has stopped
vanishing ahead
and allows us to come up close,
feel the roughness of leaf and stalk
in a lost garden,
hear the half-finished sentences
of the tall people
who sometimes answer, sometimes don't.

MORNING BRIGHTNESS

The dream house goes dark.
Everyday light is waiting to come in.
It has seen so much,
has heard so many words and it looks sad
like a poor cousin
stranded in a Victorian novel.

TOO EARLY TO REMEMBER

Above the island, they would have groaned
now and then, Spitfires, Avro Ansons.

In a manse garden on the island,
rhododendron blossoms would have sucked
what they could of the sun. In the shade
beneath leathery leaves blackbird eyes
would have missed nothing. On the steeple
lichen would have heated up all day.

In a room in an echoing house
on the island, Brahms would have been heard,
fistfuls unfolded to caresses,
caresses tightened to pack their punch,
the piano at such a distance
from that third floor flat on Karlsgasse 4.

THE FOREST BENEATH

Million-part polyphony,
wordless, for very mixed choir:
conifers and leafy trees,
young (a few decades), mature
(a couple of centuries),
the grown straight and the grown squint,
the squat, making do with shade,
the tall, tops tearing low cloud.

What about the underground,
filaments, mycelium,
the forest beneath the trees
our hearing can't let us hear?
If we could see it we'd see
a widespread metropolis
by night with circulating
headlights tiny and tireless.

FLIGHT-PATHS

Spring sky above German Bight -
but instead of Constable's
cloud masses, something more like
noughts and crosses in wet ink
spreading, noughts non-circular,
crosses going all spidery

as if Dante's universe
had lost its gravitation
and all the planes, all the rows
of humanity, went pell-
mell everyone his own way
like the scattering of sheep.

NIGHT-CROSSING

Perhaps the little I see
would count as optimistic:

perhaps eastward, a pale line
between black cloud and black sea

perhaps on a cargo-ship,
a wavering light like a remote star.

LIFE-LINES

Revisiting the Tyne
where it meets the sea
(leaving river for sea
or sea for river)
nothing like *hic jacet*
for the distant dead
nothing like street corners
to hold memories

for there's no map of here
no calendar, just
a tumultuous line
soon unturmoiling
back into the tidal
slant of the shallows.

EASTER CLOUDS

Vestments white and gold
for the death of death
while outside high walls
the heavens above
poured cold water on
that Easter Sunday
we left as we sailed
into a black east

where a Monday broke
open with swagging
clouds Blake once painted.

CUL-DE-SAC

I lose both sight and sound
of the human river.

The cobbles look as if
no-one has stepped on them
ever
and a small cloud pausing
seems to have balanced there
always.

I'm back in the river.
It's in full spate now
in a world whose compass
doesn't know where north is.

EARLY WORDS

"Pirnmill," perhaps a place-name
like "Shedog" or "Sannox," jabs
in the flow of adult talk.

"A-little-bit-of-bread-and-
no-cheese" – what yellowhammers
chirped swaying on their top twigs.

"Himmler," "Messerschmitt," almost
acclimatised, local, like
"double-daisies" and "lupins."

THE DAYS WIDEN

There can be too much brightness.
Houses drift further apart.
No-man's-spaces are glared at.
We take too long to reach home
as in dreams, arrive too late.

If darkness were a substance –
stone or sand – we could carry
a pocketful of it, so
keep our balance through summer,
temper *lux perpetua*
with an ounce of our weakness.

MANSE FOR SALE

It's now called "Kildonan Manse."
The garden is now "gardens."
Raeburn and pulley have gone.
Cold defies refurbishment.
Strath winds are still unreformed.

A DARK SIDE OF LIGHT

Restoring
the brightness of long dulled
childhood wallpaper
or titles
like *Cruden's Concordance*
on parental shelves
no longer
in that room in that house
long ago sold on

but the light,
blessing of our known world,
is not one of us.
It fingers
names and dates on gravestones
as if reading braille.
It can't read.
Its gaze is indifferent,
as cold as a gull's.

REMEMBERING MIST

Neighbourly roof-tops bulged
as high as cathedrals.
The map of our near-world
was a *mappamundi*,
approximate, with blanks.
Sparrows shuttled between
wormy fields and nest-sized
gaps in gable-end tiles.

In daytime dusk a man
stooped over a flower-bed:
something must have been lost.
As seen from my window
the universe leaned down
helping the small human.

That was long ago now
but that day never stopped.
What was lost was not found.
As seen from my window
the man and his helper
are still leaning, looking.

WHITSUN WITHOUT WORDS

Not one tongue today.
Brightness above clouds –
the stuff of rumours.

Fundamentalists
poison the airwaves.
Birch and pine send out
gentle antidotes,
pollen from the birch,
resin from the pine.

Along the fjord edge
millions of small waves
send out the same sound,
neither noun nor verb,
unmemorable
and not yet a word.
The most tolerant
of dictionaries
wouldn't give it space.

FAR AWAY IS HERE

Somewhere far away and long ago –
a reed shaken by the wind, also
purple irises in damp hollows
and buttercups and white wild roses.

The wind that ruffles my hair today
can't tell the time and can't tell the year
and doesn't know which island we're on.
Without it, I wouldn't know where I am.

A THIN BURN

The dead have a bad habit
of giving me wrong answers
to questions I haven't asked.

The questions I want to ask
swirl like crows that can't settle
for the night, not there, not yet.

A thin burn percolating
from wide heathery nowhere
gives an impression of speech.

"Never mind the dead," it says.
But next time I hear Murdo
make the world sound like Caithness

the burn has nothing to say
that doesn't sound like water,
water and only water.

EDINBURGH JULY

October haar has sidled in.
The lips around me keep moving
but their words are now too silent
for a language of the living.
If there were an hour-glass to hand
the grains would have stopped in mid-fall.

MIRACLE
(Sankt Nikolai, Flensburg)

Cathedral walls have not been anywhere.
The bricks were ordered to stay where they were,
had no inclination to disobey.

Close by, one copper-beech and two ash-trees
swell and shrink in the breeze as if they've found
the secret of perpetual motion.

Today the trees are unmoving as rock.
Cathedral walls have warm nerves, breathe like skin.

The dead soldiers listed in the big book
are found presumed alive, on their way home.

SAILING SOUTH FROM THE TYNE

For ten minutes I think I belong here,
within reach, out of reach,
ten minutes of departure, in transit,
chafe-marks on the quayside
as close as large letters on a white page,
as remote as last year.

Gulls in turmoil over swirls in turmoil
swoop mostly on nothing.
Northumbria then Yorkshire lose their weight
of rock and earth and walls,
now a haze as if from an after-life
uncertain and short-lived.

EVENING ON DECK

A thin slice of a very new moon –
at last something of substance to watch,
something that knows its place, where to go

unlike the water-coils of our wake
strangling each other, leaving smooth sea;
unlike that ochre cloud, that brush-stroke
jabbed between horizon and zenith;
unlike that fake lighthouse, small window
multiplying the harshness of sunset.

SUMMER CLOUDS

The blackest. Against them
the greenest sycamores
show up white. The fresh name
newly chipped on marble
shows up black. I've seen it
always hand-written, spidery.

TALKING TO YOU NOW

Thirty-three years of your silence.
Wouldn't you like to feel the breeze
and watch the sycamore tops sway?
Wouldn't you like to be warmed up
by the sun you won't ever see?
There must be something you might want,
uncomplicated, beyond reach.

MEMORY BOTH WAYS

They might tell me
it's my age that livens the sourness
of clay in a Clarkston back garden
after rain in 1947.

I might tell them
when I'm in 1947
I have a resinous memory
of a young spruce in young spring sunlight
on the other side of the North Sea
far back in 2017.

ÅLESUND HARBOUR

A much used surface. Not just the wind
when it chooses to assert itself
inventing endless variations
on the unstable theme of one wave
or when it pretends to be absent
yet spreads pages of vanishing text
in miniature cuneiform wedges –
but all the keels slicing their straight lines
that humans love and nature abhors.

The buildings wobble in the water.
No reason why it can't be normal
looking down at stars, not up at them.
No reason why trees can't grow earthwards,
roots in clouds. No reason why boulders
can't float like petals.

PIANO PRACTICE

Beyond gardens, higher than fields,
heather roots grasped strath and summits
as if their world had no edges.
The moor wasn't eternity.
It was just plant life going on
for as long as time allowed it.

Within four walls the air would be
disturbed for many hours a day
by sounds invented in Leipzig.
They'd hint at eternity then
having settled on a cadence
would leave a room full of silence.

HORIZON

Such crowding cumulus on the skyline
as if there's something just behind earth's curve
clouds know they should try to bulge away from

as if about-to-shrink chrysanthemums
have forgotten their age-old timetables
and seasons are losing their grip on us.

A WAVE

Remembering a good man:

as when an unobtrusive
but not to be hindered wave
arrives from a great distance,

breaks with a whisper along
many miles of sand and smooths
the confusion of footprints

which may be "likened unto"
indecisions, false turnings
and wrongs that can't be righted.

Nothing's denied, but a weight
has now lost its heaviness,
has learnt the buoyancy of

swaying tips of marram grass.

I STEP OUTSIDE, LATE

Street-lamps could be as far away as stars
and stars could be as close-by as street-lamps.

The night universe sweeps me with freshness
as of a quiet wave breaking in sunlight.

NOT AN EMBLEM

Not another emblem please
ripe for the interpreters –

I take note of the dog-rose
big enough for a small tree,
safely to the side of things,
exempt from the secateurs.
Also the convolvulus
which has climbed up the green shade
to unfold its soft trumpets.
Many white flowers, many red.

LATE QUARTET

The one world: the four players enter
the labyrinth they don't get lost in.
There's a beginning and an ending.

The other: the music never stops.
It's waiting for us all day, all night.
We have no means of forgetting it.

The closer it moves towards silence
the more it enables us to hear.
We eavesdrop on sounds not meant for us.

OCTOBER LEVELS

Nimble like demisemiquavers, high
aspen leaves
more yellow than reflections from mirrors –
the last light
of afternoon is their eternity.

We watch them from lower half-shadows where
sturdy boles
make us feel meagre and temporary.

OCTOBER'S LAST LIGHT

Yellow half-blinding me
is alive as it was
seven decades ago

when the irises sway
ruffled by Caithness air
that can't leave undisturbed

the least significant
backwater pool half-in
-out of Thurso River.

Years, transparent windows.
We look, don't know which side
is past and which present.

REMOTE

It has stayed in the same place and
followed me for sixty-five years,
something remote lochs are good at.

Seen online, nowhere is remote.
Here is the hour-by-hour forecast
for Loch Arichlinie today:

breeze gentle, rain none. Nobody
will notice the miniature waves
noticing the gentleness of the breeze.

RIVER

Seepings from a dozen peatland lochs
keeping it alive

its course nonetheless a nervous thread
of meanderings

as if to postpone
a scattering in the Pentland Firth

its freshness at last
set upon by headlong Atlantic salt.

MARGINAL

Places to the side
near where we once lived,

noticed not noticed
from a daily route –

Gartymore, Gordonbush, Rothiemurchus.

In light we walk past
book-spines in shadow,

accounted-for lives
waiting to be seen.

SEEMING

"We light dark tunnels with our eyes"
the Polish lady wrote, of dreams.

Dante made invisible things
visible by glaring at them.

The pine trees I walk among seem
wide awake in their patient way,

seem whole-heartedly in a world
of high clouds and moist forest floor,

seem to scrutinize me as if
I've never been and never shall be.

LEAVING

That's Edinburgh, then, for this time.
What can I do with these street-corners
I've "missed," apart from walking round them,
turning from Chambers Street to South Bridge,
turning from South Bridge to Chambers Street?
The city's too heavy to take home.

In a dream it was an animal
held captive for decades but keeping
still its silent non-humanity,
its stony but not unfriendly stare
that told me I had no grandparents,
no parents here, and no myself here.

FAMILY GRAVESTONES

"Occasional mild spells but mostly
below average temperatures, with rain."

If only they were as familiar
as old-fashioned mantelpieces,
tiles keeping warmth alive, and not a touch
of the loneliness of the universe.

STREET-LAMPS

When they're not shining on anyone
and the conifer wall behind them
is still as stone and no longer green
and roofs of houses and garages
say nothing as they did the day long

when they're not shining on anyone
they shed a terrible loneliness
that only utter darkness can cure.

THE LIGHT MAKER

Her kindness is to be interpreted
as light.

Now when
the sun has leant as far south as it can
she sets
out in the freezing glassed-in veranda
old-time
flickery candles and new-time led-bulbs,
as if
banishing timeless worries of the night

perhaps
only for an hour or two, even so
banishing.

SARABANDE

As if the thin burn that trickles
from little rock-pool to little
rock-pool down from Creag Scalabsdale

were to slow its pace, let me hear
each mordant and turn and cadence

as water elaborates on
the simple roundness of pebbles
and the sharpness of rock edges,

I soon imagine I'm listening
to a wide momentous waterway.

WHERE

Not behind me
not before me
not beside me
but *something* me

a dimension
too *here* for words,
least to be found
on deaf headstones

John Scott Fulton
(I smell *Capstan*)
Agnes MacLeod
(I smell *Gold Flake*)

59 PRINCES STREET

Before the drawing of curtains
wax tapers lit by Swan Vestas
would pop pent-up gas into life:
brightness enough for darning socks,
scouring *The Caithness Courier*

but always leaving dark spaces
behind looming armchairs or through
that corridor past the toilet
(lampless but illuminated faintly
by a stained-glass panel
in the door, showing Chinese boats) –

pre-electric dull recesses
like life's unhappy minutes best
forgotten but not forgotten,
and the happy minutes, brilliance
seen now encapsulated in shadow.

AT A GLANCE

Is this how divinity works –
in the dark, a pin-
point of light noticed, forgotten?

Could be a landing-light seeming
still as a star seems
but at speed sagging towards earth.

Could be a lamp-post not far off
lighting up all night
a crumbling path leading nowhere

except to a disused harbour
where the water gleams
like a surface we could walk on.

TREES WATCHING OVER US

When sunlight, moonlight and even starlight
leave us
trees we have known will gather round, concerned –
tough yes
and tolerating more life than we do
but if
they worry they must worry about age
like us.

Unable to coax us back to the light
they'll drift
slowly to the places they've always been
and if
they're in the habit of comparing things
they might
imagine they watch us the way we watch
e.g.
living-in-a-hectic-hurry sparrows.

A MORNING TO WATCH

A peaceful start to a new day.
Look once: an over-sized pale moon
has paused behind the white birches
and seems unlikely to move on.
The bedrock I share with the trees
has always been there, always will.

Look twice: the pale moon's in free fall
through space with neither up nor down
and the bedrock the white birches
share with me is turning its back
on the lost moon at frantic speed.
It can't get far enough away.

NEIGHBOURLY

Each time we look at the universe,
what we can't see of it gets bigger.

What a relief then to catch sight of
that neighbourly crow watching his world
from the topmost twig of a beech tree.

The crow must be late medieval
and the tree early medieval.
Such neighbourliness, centuries deep,
protects us from the empty light-years.

UNHEARD MUSIC

Each minim of silence contains
sixteen demisemiquavers
all of them equally silent.

To those with ears to hear, silence
in F sharp minor is remote
from silence in A flat major.

Doesn't it ever happen that
the black ovals clinging like fruit
to their taut espalier wires

melt a little as the paper
now and then almost remembers
what the rain could sound like on leaves?

THE CLOCK

Visiting places where the past happened –
the past isn't there.

The war memorial clock in Helmsdale
decade by decade
keeps slicing the same hour into quarters.

THE EYE

Well-scuffed wood or chafed leather –
that's how the road looked today
with its end of season snow.
As if somewhere cloud has thinned,
lets through something like sunlight,
a pool, no longer ice, gleams.
It's like an eye half awake
still watching its own world, where
Edinburgh, or Stockholm,
are dream versions not on maps,
always there for the dreamer,
and the dead are full of life
as if nothing has changed them.
The frail glass bridge the dreamer
is walking over gives way.
The dead don't notice his fall.
The eye is wide awake now,
the colour of today's clouds.

JUTLAND ROADSIDE

Smiling, or smiled upon, the pool
glimpsed from the motorway is ice.
It's all brilliance and all surface
painful to a hurrying eye.

A signpost to Børglum Kloster –
the monks must have stopped feeling cold
and heat four centuries ago.
Their prayers must have risen, mist
becoming ephemeral trees
unbent by prevailing west winds.
We can't tell if their prayers were
anxious questions or grateful replies.

ABOUT TO LEAVE

It could have asked me to stay on.

The old beech had so many feet
in the earth and so many hands
in the air, it was well-endowed
to linger a century more.

I had nothing against waiting
a century or more with him
but something could have made me say
that all my life I'm about to leave.

EASTER DARK

Minster doors taller than humans
were locked. Shadows were compacted
in the voluminous prison.
Clerestory windows couldn't help.

We sailed from the island that night.
Waves were black because clouds were black.

SHORT-CUT

In a much improved Sutherland
I took a new road, a new bridge
then missed what I'd wanted to see:

high on a steep hill, a locked church
with no steeple, no stained glass, left
guarding nineteenth century graves

while around it meagre seasons
did their best to be pale in spring
and more or less russet in autumn.

TIGH-NA-BRUACH

"But who are your people?" he'd ask,
that Gaelic poet who knew his
like a cab-driver needling through
the labyrinth of a London.

My people includes a green door
and a voice "It's open come in"
and an unheated front parlour
where I'm sent to fetch the whisky
back to the living-room's peat fire
that's kept alive all day all night
and a view over the river
to the other bank, the graveyard
where the family tree can be read.

GOLSPIE

December '54.
Not quite sunrise – a few shimmers
of red behind the horizon.

Rock pools on the shore look
like eyes of silent animals
who may be asleep, may not be.

FAR FROM EARTH

"Life" elsewhere, too remote, too far ahead,
not something animals bother about
and our life-spans are too brief to get there.

Birthdays in the twentieth century –
that makes us prehistoric long before
anyone sets foot on a life elsewhere

and is astonished to find a harebell
with a fresh twentieth century blue
and trembling in a mild familiar breeze.

VILLAGE

Will I go back in space, only to find
the village is now in another time?
Will I go back in time, only to find
I'm looking through thick glass and I can't breathe?

I'll drive to a village I've never seen.
When I arrive I'll set my watch at Now
and wander about for a while in Here.
There won't be a village for me to leave.

AUTOBIOGRAPHY

Stepped into the world, saw

half a translucent moon
and a worn-through cloud-wisp
equidistant from earth,
each of them the same weight.

Will the world correct me?

MY KNOWLEDGE

As far as I know
on my date of birth
pines were invented
and the wind found ways
of whishing through them.
It was about then
harebells became pale
and cornflowers dark blue.

As far as I know
is not far enough
I'll be told. But pines
and the wind in them,
harebells and cornflowers
will not survive me
by even one minute.

MIDSUMMER

Evenings are too bright and last too long.
Agoraphobia confuses
the distances I'm familiar with.
Pine trees that have lived seven decades
side by side have now moved miles apart

and even the syllables we need
let the spaces between them widen
and soon they'll lose sight of each other.
We wonder if they'll find their way back
and join into words when evenings darken.

PRESENCES

Thrawn limpets that refuse to be thumbed off
tidal rocks between Thurso and Scrabster,
the high clock-face boarded up for decades
on Miller Academy (mother's school)–

Why do these punish me with their presence?
"Long-term memory," I hear. "It's your age.
The further away things are, the clearer."

But that can't be right. Yesterday's bad news
has swollen up like a bloated full moon:
all round its edge there's no space left for sky.

1959

Foreground –
Final Honours exams, Adam House,
and wrong decisions I thought were right –
now background.

Background –
an evening song-thrush loud in George Square
and Edwin Muir's "One Foot in Eden" –
now foreground.

LANGUAGE

Why are words like stepping-stones
not there when I step on them?
I remember my passwords
but forget the word "password."
Synonyms and antonyms
change places behind my back.

Is language like Noah's ark?
Do we hope its creaking planks
will revive and put forth leaves
and welcome hundreds of doves
then defy Archimedes
and promise never to sink?

COMPANY

I drove through the shadow of roadside pines.
They insisted on staying where they were

insisted on keeping me company
all the way to the failing of daylight.

WHAT IF

it's anger not love that moves
the sun and the other stars?

The sun's fury cools façades
along late evening pavements
summer crowds have left empty.

A tiny bit of God's ire
in the shape of two birch logs
flaring down into embers
gives an hour of belonging
for the two or three gathered
to forget they don't belong.

A wavering cone of rage
at the tip of a candle
tries to remember the dead.

WOOD FIRE IN SUMMER

Have the birch logs forgotten
the sound of wind and rain on leaves
the way those who have died seem
to have lost the whole alphabet
and all the words made from it?

Outside, sunlight makes grand gestures
as if it has the last word.
Inside, the wood fire concentrates
mightily on its embers,
and the people staring at it
almost imagine they're trees
content to be rooted, hearing
wind and rain on their many leaves.

WAKING IN ALT DUVENSTEDT

In the darkness I was an empty hull
cuffed by waves that didn't know where they were.

When darkness ended the church bell woke me
to sheltering trees and sheltered roof-tops.

In the light my dream revisited me:
I was fully laden, ready to sail,
buoyant on waves that knew where to take me.

OUT OF SIGHT

Eyemouth down to Cockburnspath –
father's holiday coastline
while the First World War lingered.

Speeding now over the Eye
I fail to see the water.
It must be too far below
the layers of summer leafage.

UNBURDENING

I drop off the weight of the Old Quad,
Chambers Street, Adam House, Minto House,
Carrubber's Close, Tweeddale Court, Blackfriars Wynd –

I expect to rise to a surface
but I don't. I'm more weighed-down than ever.

HOW THE SUNLIGHT FADES

Lindisfarne Castle turns soft and black,
The Angel of the North hard and black.
The leaves around Pity Me hold out
hoping their darkest green won't turn black.
There's not much they can do about their fear
that the next dawn to come may not notice them.

BRIGHTNESS ON THE NORTH SEA

Starboard – Northumberland rock
pulverised into a haze.
Port – haze with nothing to hide.

The light doesn't miss the land
the way we do, far out here.
It has plenty to see to.

White tops too white to believe
seem to give the fading sun
a brightness it has now lost.

Half a rainbow follows us
for hours, promising nothing.
No-one is disappointed.

THE ARRAN HORSE

Distance measured in decades –
now both distance and decades
uncertain. Variations
on summer green surround me,
pine-needle green, birch-leaf green.
They don't know they're in Norway,
don't know I watch them not know.

Why is it so bluntly *here*,
this horse's muzzle steaming
in November air that reeks
of yanked-up potato haulms?
That it's 1943
by a field-end at Torbeg
is of no concern to the horse.

LATE

Late summer, late afternoon,
bringings in from the garden,
a coolness noticed, leaves now
uncertain.

A book of First World War poets
is forgotten, will be found
soft and damp when a new day
has arrived.

A RUSH

Fieldfares, probably,
hundreds, certainly.

Arrows, a black wave.
Who leads? All follow.

Into a hawthorn,
out of a hawthorn.

A whirr over me.
If the Holy Ghost
had an engine, that's
what it would sound like.

HOW STILL

How still and fragile and pale blue
in a half-light clearer than noon.
One small cloud moving, not moving,
making no sound that we can hear.
Leaves have been undisturbed all night.
Their life-expectancy seems good.

So what makes me think of tremors
light-years away, as if close by,
melting down worlds, leaving deserts
where a leaf can't be invented?

21 MINIATURES

FEBRUARY

A pool where no pool should be
in a field of thin green mist.

The pool is a pale blue eye.

The thin mist hopes to be dense.
The eye doesn't want to close.

PAUSE

September plant life, at its richest.
This morning however the sun's rays
reach down to us the way they reach down
through cloudy fathoms of the deep.

LÜBECK IN THE RAIN

The saxophone man
spreads melancholy. Church bells
punch holes in the mist.

LÜBECK IN THE SUN

The accordion player
pushes and pulls into life
a cathedral-sized Bach fugue.

Now and then a passerby
half stops as if recalling
how a brisk stream meets a stone.

LIGHT ON THE NORTH SEA

Like a beginning.
Or like an ending.

Coppery sunlight
spills without wasting.

Round wave-backs rounding:
darkness won't stop them.

TOO SOON FOR LIGHT

Water in the harbour's still
a concentrate of darkness.

Wakened gulls sound like chisels
as if chipping at marble.

REMEMBERING CLOUDS

It could be Emil Nolde
or perhaps it was Paul Klee
who remembered those cloud shapes

that drifted into, out of
one evening a million years
at least before they were born.

FRÜHLINGSRAUSCHEN

Such crowding of daffodils –
they seem optimistic.
Such thickness of clouds hiding
the brilliance above them.
Behind the roar of bare trees
waves roar against bare rock.

NEWCOMERS

Our Adam and Eve
exhilaration
tells us we're the first to use human eyes.

The pines might well shrug:
What's the fuss about?
How long do you think we've been swishing mist?

NEIGHBOUR

The ruffled willow –
the white makes the green greener,
the green makes the white whiter.

The willow I watch
was once hacked down to a stump.
Today's white and green is a river.

DECADES

The straw dust thick in the air
of that rank Arran farmyard
still chokes me after decades.

The warmth in my finger-tips
from that dyke of Caithness flags –
stone has forgotten to cool.

RECOVERY

Those stone lumps dumped on my cairn
are now weightless in the breeze
like nimble heads of cotton-grass.

WAKING, EN ROUTE

Wet tyres on the M62.
Black waves bludgeoning ship's metal.
A pigeon with only one phrase.

Each dawn has its sound, but the dreams
lift off silently, birds of prey
losing interest in their booty.

FROM AN UPPER DECK

The patient engines churn out frothing curls
with a life-span of about two minutes.
On the passing coast pine trees demonstrate
how they keep their balance for centuries
with roots like wire welded into thin cracks.
The skerries with no trees are waiting still.

AFTER A DROUGHT

Curtains remember how to sway,
willows how to swish
in the half light long before dawn.

The puddle beneath the lamp-post
has returned at last.
It's my eye on the wider world.

SAFE MORNING

Without a doubt –
today opens for all souls in Alt Duvenstedt,
the chimes a laying-on of hands.
Sheltering trees will still shelter every roof-ridge –
even with doubt.

VERY EARLY

Chimney shadows on roof-tiles –
blurred, unnaturally long.

Hortensias now side-lit –
pale stems we don't see by day.

Trees still packed tight with summer –
saved-up envelopes of darkness.

SENSES

I'm held together by five.
Another, sixth or seventh,
I didn't grow up with, tilts
me. This familiar pavement sways.
It's a swing bridge above a river.

AFTER A STORM

What a blaze between black clouds
low in the west.
Perhaps a father figure.
Perhaps a mother figure.
I can't tell what I'm given,
admonition or forgiveness.

LOCKED IN

The shadows that spend all day
wavering in cathedrals
are not allowed to go out.
There are fears that tall shadows
may turn into deep black wells
where sunlit memories sink.

SPIRE

Briefly, birch leaves are all light.
Starling wings too are all light.

The spire's needle-point is high.
The spire tells us how stone lasts.

It might have preferred to be
made all of light, and short-lived.

Afterword

REMEMBERING ÖSTEN SJÖSTRAND

In Mariefred we spent days
rearranging verbs in the gap
between languages.
Autumn around us was so rich
our languages became poorer.
Jagged years waited.

Decades later from a high deck
out in the Kattegat I see
a horizon-thread:
that's his Bohuslän. When life turned
jagged his imagination
tugged him away down
into underwater forests.
He heard liberating music
where the rest of us
would be deafened by Rapture of the Deep.